MARIO ANDRETTI

RACE CAR LEGENDS

COLLECTOR'S EDITION

A.J. Foyt

The Allisons

Dale Earnhardt Jr.

Danica Patrick

Famous Finishes

Famous Tracks

The Jarretts

Jeff Burton

Jeff Gordon

Jimmie Johnson

Kenny Irwin Jr.

The Labonte Brothers

Lowriders

Mario Andretti

Mark Martin

Monster Trucks & Tractors

Motorcycles

The Need for Speed

Off-Road Racing

The Pit Crew

Rockcrawling

Rusty Wallace

Stunt Driving

Tony Stewart

The Unsers

MARIO ANDRETTI

G.S. Prentzas

CHELSEA HOUSE
PUBLISHERS

An imprint of Infobase Publishing

Mario Andretti

Chelsea House
An imprint of Infobase Publishing
132 West 31st Street
New York NY 10001

ISBN-10: 0-7910-8755-7
ISBN-13: 978-0-7910-8755-8

Library of Congress Cataloging-in-Publication Data
Prentzas, G.S.
  Mario Andretti / G.S. Prentzas.
    p. cm. – (Race car legends. Collector's edition)
Includes bibliographical references and index.
ISBN 0-7910-8755-7
1. Andretti, Mario, 1940—Juvenile literature. 2. Automobile racing drivers—United States—Biography—Juvenile literature. I. Title. II. Series.
  GV1032.A5P742 2006   796.72'092—dc22
  [B] 2005020276

Chelsea House books are available at special discounts when purchased in bulk quantities for businesses, associations, institutions, or sales promotions. Please call our Special Sales Department in New York at (212) 967-8800 or (800) 322-8755.

You can find Chelsea House books on the World Wide Web at
http://www.chelseahouse.com

Series design by Erika K. Arroyo
Cover design by Hierophant Publishing Services/EON PreMedia/Joo Young An

Printed in the United States of America

BANG PH 10 9 8 7 6 5 4 3 2 1

This book is printed on acid-free paper.

All links and Web addresses were checked and verified to be correct at the time of publication. Because of the dynamic nature of the Web, some addresses and links may have changed since publication and may no longer be valid.

CONTENTS

1

▨▨▨▨▨▨

VICTORY AT THE BRICKYARD

On May 30, 1969, the crowd filled every seat in the grandstands and infield at the Indianapolis Motor Speedway. They were eager to witness the annual running of the greatest spectacle in auto racing, the Indianapolis 500. Across the United States, nearly one million people jammed into theaters to watch a television broadcast of the event.

Drivers, crews, and car owners grew restless as the clock slowly ticked toward 11:00 A.M., the official starting time of the race. The 33 cars were lined up in a starting grid made of 11 rows, three cars to a row. In the first row were the drivers who had set the three fastest speeds during a four-lap **qualifying round** run earlier in the week. The car of three-time Indy 500 winner A.J. Foyt sat on the inside of the front row. In his Ford-powered Coyote, Foyt had blistered the track at 170.568 mph to capture the **pole position**. Bobby Unser was positioned on the outside of the front row. He had won the 1968 Indy 500 and was the defending United States Auto Club (USAC) national champion.

Bobby Unser, Mario Andretti, and A.J. Foyt *(left to right)* are off to a flying start as they lead the group of 33 drivers around the first turn of the 1969 Indianapolis 500.

Standing between these two top drivers was Mario Andretti. It was a miracle that the two-time USAC national champion was even competing in this race. Most spectators had counted on the 29-year-old driver to win the pole position. The speedway's grandstands and garage areas had been abuzz after he turned **laps** at 171 miles per hour (mph) in his powerful new four wheel–drive Lotus. On race day, however, Andretti would be driving an older two wheel–drive Hawk, a much less powerful car.

On May 21, Andretti had been flying around the track on a practice run. When he emerged from the fourth turn, the rear end of the Lotus collapsed. The right rear wheel broke off, the car spun around one-and-a-half times, and it skidded 320 feet into a concrete wall. Pieces of the car flew in every direction and it burst into flames. The Lotus scraped along the wall for another 60 feet before finally grinding to a halt in the middle of the track. Andretti quickly jumped out of the burning wreckage. At the racetrack's field hospitals, doctors treated him for burns on his upper lip, nose, and cheeks. Except for the burns, Andretti had escaped from the crash without any other injuries.

The next day, Andretti calmly drove his back-up car, the Ford-powered Hawk, through the qualifying run. He secured the second spot on the starting grid. As he stood beside his car on race day, the scars from the burns were still visible on his face.

Andretti, Foyt, Unser, and the other 30 drivers had only one goal in mind as they stood beside their cars: winning the Indy 500. The race offered more than double the prize money of any other car race. And after the race, the winner could make millions of dollars by being a spokesperson for a company, or by appearing as a speaker at special events. The three demanding hours of driving would take place in front of thousands of spectators. More people watch the Indy 500 in person than any other sporting event in the United States—more than the Kentucky Derby, the Super Bowl, or the World Series. Millions of fans flock to the speedway during the month of May to watch practices. More than 350,000 spectators jam into the speedway on race day.

The burns on Andretti's face are evident as he talks to reporters about his spectacular one-car crash. His Lotus Ford broke a rear wheel, hit a wall, and burst into flames during practice at the Indianapolis Speedway.

The temperature was expected to climb up to 85°F (about 30°C) during the race. Temperatures inside the cockpit of each car would soar to about 125°F (51°C). The

THE BRICKYARD

The Indianapolis Motor Speedway hosted its first 500-mile race in 1911. Its dirt track had been paved with 3.2 million bricks two years earlier. The original bricks remain under the asphalt that now covers the 2.5-mile oval. A 36-inch strip of the original brick remains at the starting line. In addition to the Indianapolis 500, the speedway also hosts two other major races. NASCAR's Brickyard 400 has been held in August since 1994. The U.S. Grand Prix has been run at the track since 2000.

Mario Andretti (*top*), son Michael (*center*), and grandson Marco line up at the famous yard of bricks before taking a lap around the track to open practice for the 2006 Indianapolis 500.

drivers and crews awaited their cue from Tony Hulman, the owner of the speedway since 1945. Hulman's voice, amplified through loudspeakers, echoed throughout the speedway. He carefully sounded the phrase that has become synonymous with the Indy 500: "Gentlemen, start your engines."

The drivers steered their cars around the track in perfect formation during the warm-up laps. As they came out of the fourth turn on the final warm-up, the race began. The cars rocketed down the front stretch and into the first turn. Jamming the accelerator to the floorboard, Andretti nosed his car past Foyt's and into the lead. Biographer

Bill Libby recorded Andretti's comments about the 1969 Indianapolis 500. Recalling the start of the race, Andretti said, "I just accelerated normally and was surprised no one ran faster."

Although Andretti led the pack, he had little confidence that he would win. In the practice runs after qualifying, the car had been overheating. He decided to drive the car to its limit to see how much stress the engine could take. Andretti later explained, "I felt maybe after twenty, twenty-five laps it would be all over for me."

As expected, after a few laps the dashboard instruments showed that the engine was overheating. He quickly adjusted his speed to decrease the stress on the engine. On the fifth lap, Foyt zoomed past him. Soon, Foyt's teammate, Roger McCluskey, also passed him. Andretti took it easy for a while, trying to find the right speed. "I found that when the water gauge got to 220 degrees and the oil to 240, it sort of leveled off," he later recounted. "And I could hold it in balance there as long as I didn't run faster, which was around 165 [mph], and I just had to hope that was fast enough."

Foyt was out front, flying around the track. McCluskey held onto second. "It was quite a temptation to race them," Andretti recalled. "But I kept telling myself I didn't dare to." Meanwhile, the other drivers were trying to catch the leaders. Bobby Unser, after being third at the starting line, was having mechanical problems with his car. Lloyd Ruby, who had started in twentieth place, was charging up through the pack. On the fortieth lap, Ruby easily passed Andretti and McCluskey to move into second. Eight laps later, McCluskey coasted off the track for an unplanned refueling stop. By the time he got back on the track he had lost his chance for the **checkered flag**.

Andretti made his first **pit stop** on lap 52. When he pulled back onto the track, he was well behind Ruby and much farther behind Foyt. But it was not to be Foyt's day. On the seventy-ninth lap, Foyt began having engine problems. He pulled over for a pit stop, and his crew worked quickly to fix the trouble. He rejoined the race 24 minutes later, but he was too far behind the leaders to win the race.

Andretti streaked into the lead at one point when he passed Ruby. But after having to make another refueling stop, Andretti was again far behind. The crucial moment in the race came on lap number 108, when Ruby refueled. His crew chief mistakenly signaled him to take off before a refueling hose was disconnected from the car. When Ruby punched the accelerator, the hose ripped out the car's fuel tank.

Suddenly Andretti led the race. Several of the fastest cars had dropped out of the running and the closest competitors were well behind him. But the race was not over, by any means. There was still a long way to go—more than 200 miles. If anyone started pressing him, he would be forced to increase his speed. A higher speed might cause the engine to overheat or the car to run out of fuel.

Andretti kept a steady pace of 165 mph, but he was all over the track. His crew grew more anxious every time he passed slower cars. On lap number 150, as he entered the third turn, he got caught in a swirl of air whipping around another car. The force of air pushed the Hawk out of control. Fans gasped in unison. "I was sleeping out there, too relaxed," Andretti later acknowledged. "I didn't expect what happened and it startled me, and the car got out of control and started to slide up into the wall. I was sure I was going to hit the wall . . . but I steered like crazy and somehow I got it back into control."

At last, Andretti saw the **white flag**, which meant that he was going into lap number 200, the final lap. The crowd stood and cheered him on. He guided the car through the third and fourth turns. He passed the wall that he had crashed into only nine days earlier. As he crossed the finish line, Andretti had completed the 500 miles in 3 hours, 11 minutes, and 41 seconds.

When Andretti steered his bright red car into Victory Lane, his team's owner, Andy Granatelli, was waiting for him. The 300-pound bearlike man wrapped his arms around the tiny Andretti and kissed him several times on the cheek. Andretti's wife, Dee Ann, his parents, and his twin brother, Aldo, joined in the celebration.

Following the excitement in Victory Lane, Andretti met with reporters. When asked about the burns on his face, the weary driver replied, "I guess it hurts, but I was too busy to think about it until now." He discussed the race and how difficult it had been to resist driving all out. He described how he almost lost it on lap 150. Andretti admitted that he probably would not have won if a faster car had forced him to drive the Hawk at higher speeds. A reporter asked the new Indy 500 champion if he might retire. Andretti looked shocked. "No," he retorted. "I'm a race-driver, and I'm going to go on driving races."

True to his words, Andretti kept on racing. He never again won an Indy 500 race, but he did come close several times. During his brilliant career, Andretti drove anything on four wheels: midget cars, sprint cars, stock cars, and

A reporter tries to get a statement as Mario Andretti receives a kiss from jubilant car owner Andy Granatelli after a victory in the 1969 Indianapolis 500. Fans and crewmembers gather around to congratulate Andretti.

Formula 1 racers. He matched his skills and nerve with other drivers on dirt tracks, paved tracks, and road courses. No matter what kind of car, what kind of race, what kind of track, Andretti drove to win.

2

A HARD ROAD

Mario Andretti was born on February 28, 1940. Five hours later, his twin brother, Aldo, arrived. The twins grew up in Montona, a small Italian town of 3,500 people. It was typical of many small villages in Italy. At that time, donkey carts and horses moved slowly along its cobblestone streets. The village had barely any automobile traffic.

GROWING UP IN ITALY AND YUGOSLAVIA

The Andretti family was well off compared to many of their neighbors. They owned land, and Mario's father, Alvise Luigi "Gigi" Andretti, managed several local farms. Mario's mother, Rina, took care of the twins and their older sister, Anna Maria. Life was simple and fulfilling for the Andrettis until disaster struck.

That disaster was World War II. It shattered the family's life. When Germany invaded Poland in September 1939, England and France immediately declared war on Germany. Italy entered the war in June 1940 when its dictator, Benito Mussolini, sided with Germany. In 1941,

Mario stands above the Andretti family in this snapshot taken shortly before they emigrated to the United States. The Andrettis were just one of many Italian families on the Istrian Peninsula that decided to relocate after World War II, when the Italian government surrendered their homeland to Yugoslavia.

Japan joined Germany, Italy, and the other countries that made up a group called the Axis nations. That same year, the Soviet Union and the United States joined

England, France, and many other countries in opposition to the Axis powers. Their group was known as the Allies.

The war tore apart life throughout Europe. Although no battles were fought in Montona, the war still devastated the village. Goods and supplies went to support Italy's war efforts. Shortages in everything became the way of life for all Italians, including the Andrettis.

In 1944, the Allies marched over Italy on their way to Germany. The German government surrendered on May 7, 1945, and the war in Europe was finally over. Just when it appeared that the Andretti family could begin to piece their lives back together, another misfortune struck. In its surrender to the Allies, the Italian government agreed to give up the Istrian Peninsula, a thin finger of land in northeastern Italy where Montona was located. The territory was handed over to the country of Yugoslavia, Italy's neighbor to the east. Suddenly all the people living on the peninsula, mostly Italians, were citizens of Yugoslavia. Many Italians, including the Andrettis, were very worried.

In 1948, Yugoslavia gave the Italians living on the Istrian Peninsula a chance to return to Italy. Concluding that there was no future for their three children in Yugoslavia, Mario's parents decided to leave everything they had and take their family to Italy. The Andrettis ended up in a refugee camp in Lucca, which is located about 45 miles from the city of Florence. To Mario and Aldo, the camp was a great adventure. There were many other children to play with. The twins soon found an idol: their uncle, Bruno Benvegnu, who also lived in the camp. A veteran of the Italian Air Force, Benvegnu was handsome and swaggering. He let Mario and Aldo roar around the camp with him on his motorcycle.

Motovun, Croatia, formerly known as Montona, Italy, sits atop a hill on the Istrian Peninsula. The town of Andretti's birth became part of Yugoslavia after World War II. The Istrian Peninsula, which juts into the Adriatic Sea, later became part of Croatia when civil wars caused the dissolution of Yugoslavia in the 1990s.

LEARNING TO DRIVE

Gigi and Rina Andretti were not surprised that their sons loved motorcycles. Mario and Aldo's sister, Anna Maria, later recalled that the twins would pick up plates off their high chairs and pretend that they were car steering wheels. A few years later, the youngsters' great-uncle would build them a wooden car similar to a soapbox derby racer. Mario and Aldo would tear down the steep hills of Montona in their car, terrorizing neighbors who barely had room to escape on the narrow streets.

It did not take the twins very long before they found a way to be near cars. Mario and Aldo talked the owners of a Lucca garage into letting them park cars. The 13-year-olds had never driven a car before and could barely see over the dashboard. Nevertheless, Mario and Aldo zoomed through the streets of Lucca, taking cars from the central plaza to the parking garage.

The twins were soon hooked on motor vehicles. All the boys talked about were cars, motorcycles, and racing. Mario and Aldo soon found a new idol—the legendary Italian racing star Alberto Ascari. Many Italians worship race car drivers the same way that Americans idolize baseball, basketball, and football players. But at home, the Andretti boys had to be careful. Their father hated hearing any mention of auto racing, thinking it was foolish. The boys hid racing magazines under their bed so their father would not find them.

ANDRETTI'S BIG BREAK

Good fortune soon shone on the two would-be car racers. A promoter by the name of Count Giovanni Lurani devised a new racing organization that he called Formula Junior. He wanted to give young drivers, ages 14 to 21, the chance to race smaller, less powerful versions of Grand Prix (later known as Formula 1) cars. The cars would be a little bigger than go-karts. Lurani persuaded the Italian government to finance the operation, arguing that it was the best way to train a new generation of Italian racing champions. "It was a sort of Little League of auto racing, incredibly dangerous," Andretti later recalled. "Naturally Aldo and I wanted a part of it. They were accepting drivers of fourteen years of age or older. We were thirteen. We lied to get in."

Even after Mario and Aldo were admitted to the program, they had a problem—no car. Again, good fortune was on their side. One of the owners of the garage where they worked had bought a Formula Junior car for his son to drive. When the teen showed no interest in racing, Mario and Aldo cheerfully volunteered as drivers.

Behind the wheel of the Stanguelini Formula Junior car, powered by an 85-horsepower Fiat Topolino engine, Mario and Aldo began entering and winning Formula Junior races. They took turns driving and had a grand time. All the while, the twins kept their racing a secret from their father. They claimed they were going off to Boy Scout camps on weekends. When Aldo burned his fingers while playing with the engine, the twins told their parents that a box of matches had exploded in his hands. When Mario broke a kneecap in a crash, he claimed that he had fallen on some church steps.

In 1954, Mario and Aldo went to see the Grand Prix race at Monza, Italy. It proved to be a momentous trip. The Andrettis cheered loudly as their hero Ascari outdueled driver Juan Manuel Fangio, from Argentina, in an electrifying wheel-to-wheel race. "We stood at the end of the straight as it turned into a corner," Mario recalled. "I'd never been able to express it completely, but you can imagine what it meant to me to be that close. Before that time I wanted to be a race driver. After that time, I *had* to be a race driver."

Meanwhile, life for the family was tough. The Andrettis were living off welfare money from the government, in addition to what little money Gigi Andretti made at

Race cars including a Mercedes on the far left and a Ferrari in the middle wait on the starting line for the beginning of the 1954 Grand Prix in Monza, Italy.

part-time jobs. To keep their options open, the family had applied for permission to emigrate to the United States. Rina Andretti's brother, Tony Benvegnu, lived in the United States at the time. One day, the family was suddenly granted their permit. Mario and Aldo were crushed when they heard that they were moving. They believed that they would not be able to pursue their dream of racing glory in the United States. As the family began to pack for their trip, Mario and Aldo made a pact to return to Italy when they were old enough and resume their racing careers.

RACING IN THE UNITED STATES

The Italian ocean liner *Conte Biancamano* sailed from the city of Genoa with the Andrettis aboard. On the morning of June 16, 1955, the ship steamed into New York Harbor

THE LIFE OF ALBERTO ASCARI

Andretti's hero, Alberto Ascari (1918–1955), had racing in his blood. Alberto's father, Grand Prix champion Antonio Ascari (1888–1925), died when he crashed while at the lead of the rain-drenched 1925 French Grand Prix. Despite losing his father to racing, Alberto was drawn to the sport. He began racing motorcycles competitively at age 18. He switched to cars four years later and was soon driving—and winning—for the legendary Alfa Romeo team. In 1949, he became the lead driver for Ferrari. Behind the wheel of the early Ferraris, Ascari became the top driver on the Formula 1 circuit. He was world champion in 1952 and 1953 and won the Mille Miglia, Italy's famous road race, in 1954. Charming and modest, Ascari became a favorite of race fans worldwide and a celebrated national hero in Italy. In an eerie coincidence, Alberto Ascari died on May 26, 1955, when he crashed while testing a new Ferrari. His father had died on the same day 30 years earlier.

Ferrari driver Alberto Ascari, an early inspiration to the Andretti brothers, is shown on pole position before the 1953 British Grand Prix at Silverstone, England.

and past the Statue of Liberty. The Andretti family settled in Nazareth, Pennsylvania, where Tony Benvegnu had lived since 1909. Gigi Andretti quickly found work in a textile mill.

Mario and Aldo were unhappy in Nazareth. They could speak only a few words of English. Their dream of racing heroics seemed an ocean away. The twins moped around for a week until they made an exciting discovery: Nazareth had a racetrack! "That was probably the happiest moment of my life," Mario Andretti later remarked in an article in a 1992 issue of *Sports Illustrated* magazine. "Instead of looking at racing as something that was way down the road for us, this was something we could begin work on right away."

The Nazareth Speedway was a dirt oval of one-half mile. It looked nothing like the winding, paved road courses in Europe. Instead of the flashy race cars that the twins were used to seeing in Italy, **stock cars**—large American passenger cars modified for racing—noisily sped around the Nazareth track. This American style of racing was certainly less glamorous than European Grand Prix racing, but that didn't matter to Mario and Aldo. It was still racing.

Although their racing dreams had been rekindled, Mario and Aldo faced some hard realities in adjusting to life in their new home. Because of their difficulties with English, the 15-year-old twins were placed in the seventh grade with classmates who were two years younger. The following year, Mario and Aldo were nearly 17 years old and still in junior high.

A teacher recommended that the twins take at-home courses to earn their high school degrees. Mario took the advice and enrolled in a correspondence course—one in which he received his lessons and instruction by mail. He grew close to one of his instructors, Dee Ann Hoch, and they began dating. It took Mario several years to earn his high school diploma. He later commented that he would not recommend correspondence courses to other students. He felt that by not going to a real high school, he missed out on many important experiences.

3

LEARNING THE ROPES

Mario and Aldo began to work hard to make their racing dreams come true. They could not afford to buy a race car, so they decided to build one. It took them three years to learn everything they needed to know about American cars and racing. They hung out at a local garage. They went to as many races as they could afford. They fired endless questions at anyone who knew anything about race cars. They began raising funds to get the car ready. Some of the "investors" in the Andretti race team were friends who chipped in a whopping $5 apiece, not a small amount of money for many young people at that time. A $350 loan from a local bank also helped.

The first race car that the Andrettis built was made out of a 1948 Hudson Hornet. When the 1959 season at Nazareth Speedway opened on April 25, the twins realized that they still had a problem. "One car, two of us," recalled Aldo. "We decided to flip a coin for who would take the first race, and we would take turns after that." Aldo won the coin toss and jumped behind the wheel. Starting in the

The Hudson Hornet dominated stock car racing throughout the early 1950s, consistently beating cars powered by larger, more modern engines. Stock car driver Jack McGrath is shown here leaning against a battered 1953 Hudson Hornet.

back of the grid, Aldo blew past the rest of the cars to win the race. The Andrettis gleefully ran to the pay window to receive their winnings—$90. The next week, Mario guided the Hornet around the track to win the race again. The twins rang up another $90.

The Andretti boys kept winning races, but track officials soon decided to move them up to a more competitive class. They raced well but did not win in the higher class. Mario later admitted that they did not have enough experience to be driving at the speeds they were reaching.

CARING FOR A BROTHER

The final race of the 1959 season at Hatfield, Pennsylvania, was a 50-mile race. In a qualification heat, Aldo was in third place when disaster struck. Going all out to catch the leaders, Aldo caught the car on a guardrail. The Hudson tumbled end over end down the track. When Mario reached the car, Aldo was unconscious.

An ambulance raced Aldo to a local hospital. Mario was terrified. He was unsure whether Aldo would live. He was terrified at the thought of having to tell his parents about the accident. When their father heard the news, he was livid. He said that Mario and Aldo had made the family look bad. Returning to the hospital the next day, Mario learned that his brother's condition had worsened. He had slipped into a coma, and X-rays revealed that he had a skull fracture.

Mario stayed at Aldo's bedside. After two weeks Aldo's eyelash started moving, and he soon opened his eyes and became a little livelier. He joked that he was glad Mario was the one who had to tell their father about the accident. After another month, Aldo was well enough to return home, but he was still in bad shape. Aldo left the hospital weighing only 90 pounds, 70 pounds less than he had weighed six weeks earlier, and he had to relearn how to walk and write.

In the meantime, Mario had salvaged some of the parts from the crunched-up Hudson and installed them on a 1937 Hudson chassis. Gigi Andretti saw the boys hanging out with their new race car at a local garage. When they returned home that day, he told the twins that they could continue living in the house but that he would not speak to them. He was true to his word. For six months, he refused to talk to his sons.

The tension at home upset Mario, but not enough to keep him from racing. At the beginning of the 1960 season, he had four straight wins. Then Aldo announced that he was ready to race again. Mario felt that his brother had not fully recovered and tried to talk him out of returning so soon, but Aldo was adamant that he could do it.

In Aldo's first race, Mario immediately saw that his brother was having trouble controlling the car. In what seemed like a recurring nightmare, Mario watched helplessly as Aldo again hooked onto a guardrail. When the car went airborne and tumbled end over end, Mario felt sure that his brother was done for. Yet, Aldo emerged from the wreckage with only a bloody finger, and agreed that he should take it easy for a while.

A RACING CAREER ADVANCES

While Aldo stood on the sidelines, Mario's racing career began to advance. Just like baseball's major and minor leagues, auto racing also has different leagues of skill. Drivers usually start racing motorcycles or sports cars and slowly work their way up to more competitive forms of racing. Mario started working his way up on small tracks throughout the Northeast and the Midwest.

In 1960, Mario began driving a stock car sponsored by a construction company. He also got involved in **sprint car** racing, which was a big step up in his career. His first sprint car ride was in a racer from the late 1940s that had a Cadillac engine and practically no brakes. He finished in eighth place in his first sprint race.

Aldo Andretti *(far left)* sits next to Mario and other race crewmembers on a trackside wall in this undated photo.

During 1960 and 1961, Andretti entered 46 stock car races and won 21—a strong performance. But on the more difficult United Racing Club (URC) sprint car **circuit**, he managed to finish only about half of the 20 races that he entered. Although he wasn't winning any races, he was gaining a lot of experience.

He also wanted to drive bigger and better cars, but no one would give him a chance. He soon figured out the problem—car owners thought that he was too small. Many people in the racing world believed that drivers had to be big, strong men to handle powerful racers. Andretti was constantly given inferior cars because owners did not trust the scrawny 21-year-old with their best cars. In a few years, however, Andretti's size—5 feet, 5 inches tall and 135 pounds—would become an advantage. Races began to be dominated by cars with engines in the rear. Those kinds of cars have very small cockpits, and so they are best raced by small drivers.

Meanwhile, the relationship between Andretti and his old high school teacher, Dee Ann Hoch, blossomed. The couple married on November 25, 1961. With financial help from his father-in-law, Andretti bought a three-quarter **midget racer** and began racing in indoor races during the winter.

Midget car racing is chaotic. Many cars compete in each round, and the packed track always becomes a mess of spins and crashes as the cars dash toward the finish line. At first, Andretti did not do very well on the midget circuit, but he eventually won his first race on March 3, 1962. The victory in the 35-lap race in Teaneck, New Jersey, boosted his confidence. He won three more races before the end of the season.

Andretti did not make much money, but he was beginning to build a reputation for himself. His performance on the midget circuit attracted the notice of Bill and Eddie

Mario Andretti gazes down the track as he waits beside the midget racer that he drove for the Mataka brothers during the 1963 racing season.

Mataka. The Mataka brothers owned a racing team based in Maplewood, New Jersey. They asked Andretti to drive their Offenhauser midget racer for the 1962 summer season. Andretti accepted the offer and won his first midget race of the year. He drove about 80 midget races for the Mataka brothers in 1963, but Andretti was not satisfied. He was still in the minor leagues. When a better opportunity came along, he left the Mataka team.

On September 21, 1963, Andretti drove in his first United States Auto Club (USAC) race, a sprint car race in Allentown, Pennsylvania. He competed against A.J. Foyt and other top drivers. Andretti was the fourth fastest driver in the qualifying round. In the main event race, however, the brakes on his car stopped working, and he finished in fourteenth place. In a race two weeks later,

SPRINT CARS

Sprint car racing is one of the oldest types of motor sports in the United States. It is also perhaps the most dangerous. The small cars have powerful engines and are very easy to maneuver. The races are usually run on dirt tracks that get bumpy after the racers have completed a few laps. The lightweight cars easily go airborne when they hit a ditch. Many drivers have been killed in sprint car races. Today, there are many regional sprint car racing circuits throughout the country. The most well known circuits are the All-Star Circuit of Champions, the Sprint Car Racing Association, and the World of Outlaws.

Andretti finished in thirteenth place. He was not thrilled with the poor finishes, but he comforted himself with the knowledge that he had gotten the most out of the car. He savored the first taste of competition against the big guys of USAC. Andretti was one step closer to the big time.

CHAMPIONSHIP RACES

In April 1964, Andretti got an offer to drive in the Trenton 100. It would be his first USAC championship race—the major leagues of U.S. auto racing. The Trenton oval was paved, a real treat for the young driver after having driven on bumpier dirt tracks. On race day, however, a light rain that kept coming and going made conditions on the smooth asphalt extremely treacherous. This was especially true for Andretti, who was behind the wheel of a car with poor brakes. He labored home in eleventh place.

Andretti anxiously awaited a call to drive in the 1964 Indianapolis 500, but his telephone did not ring. It was beginning to look as if he would be returning to the minor leagues, when one day he received a call from Rufus Gray, a respected car owner. He asked Andretti if he would be interested in driving one of Gray's sprint cars. Andretti knew that this opportunity could be a turning point in his career. If things worked out, he could become a full-time driver.

Andretti's first sprint car race with Gray was to be a big event on a dirt track in Salem, Indiana. The race was scheduled for May 3, but heavy rain forced its cancellation. Andretti returned to Indiana at the end of the month to

Mario Andretti runs the number 2 Overseas National Airways Kuzma Offy sprint car in the 1968 Hoosier Hundred, a race held at the Indiana State Fairgrounds in Indianapolis, Indiana. Known as the "Track of Champions" because of the many great drivers who raced there over the years, this one-mile dirt oval may be the oldest continuously operating auto racing track in the United States.

attend the 1964 Indy 500 as a spectator. He realized that he was not ready to compete at the Brickyard yet, but he wanted to look, listen, and learn.

The rescheduled Salem race was finally run, and Andretti finished in fourth place. It turned out that he was in the right place at the right time. Legendary crew chief Clint Brawner was looking for a driver for his championship car. In a sprint car race in Terre Haute, Indiana, Brawner watched the young kid from Nazareth duel A.J. Foyt. The older driver won the race, but Andretti was still impressive.

Brawner asked him to join the Dean Van Lines team. He wanted Andretti to take it easy at first—so he could learn the ropes. Andretti's first race with the Dean Van Lines team was the Trenton 150. He was running in sixth place when he hit an oil slick on lap 78. The car spun wildly, but Andretti avoided hitting anything. He got the car started again and finished in eleventh place. At the next race in the circuit, the Milwaukee 200, he finished third.

Between stops on the championship circuit, Andretti continued driving in the USAC National Sprint Car division. All season long, he had been finishing near the front in the Rufus Gray car but had not captured a single checkered flag. Then on October 4, he won his first sprint car race—a 50-mile race in Salem, Indiana. He and the crew celebrated his first USAC victory.

By the end of the 1964 season, Andretti had finished in the top 10 in 5 races. He had picked up enough points to finish eleventh in the USAC championship point race. It was a remarkable feat because he had not raced for the entire season. To top off his impressive rookie year, he finished third in the USAC sprint car standings.

4

THE BIG TIME

Going into the 1965 season, Andretti worried that he would lose his job. He had joined Brawner's operation as a substitute driver. Because of his success, however, he felt that he should be Dean Van Lines's full-time driver. He presented his demands to Brawner, who agreed to keep Andretti as his sole driver. The young driver would receive $5,000 per year and earn 40 percent of the winnings.

RACING AS A ROOKIE

In the first race of the season, the Phoenix 150, Andretti led the race for 63 laps. It was the first time he had ever been in front in a USAC championship race. But on lap 110, while trying to avoid Johnny Rutherford's spinning car, he lost the lead to Don Branson and ended up finishing in sixth place. At the next race, the Trenton 100, Andretti finished second behind Jim McElreath.

The next major race on the USAC calendar was the biggest race of them all—the Indianapolis 500. The month-long preparation for the race always drains drivers and their crews. Tension mounts with each passing day, especially for rookie drivers. Andretti was not the only hot-shot rookie driver who showed up at the Brickyard in

Mario Andretti started out the 1965 season as Dean Van Lines's full-time driver. He is shown here in the number 12 Ford, which was owned by Clint Brawner.

1965. Gordon Johncock, Al Unser, and Mickey Rupp also arrived for their first try at Indy.

Rookie drivers must pass a rookie test before they are even allowed to run in the qualifying rounds. Andretti had no trouble with the test and passed it with flying colors. But next came the really hard part—qualifying for the race. Only 33 cars can run in the Indy 500, but about 70 cars usually compete during the four days of qualifying.

Andretti, the eleventh driver to take the track, quickly made a name for himself by posting a 158.849 mph time, breaking the track record. But three other drivers later posted better times. Still, Andretti was overjoyed with his effort. Not only had he qualified for the race, but also he would be starting in the second row behind the top three drivers.

From his fourth-place start, Andretti soon realized that he could not keep up with the two fastest cars. But he did feel that he could outrun the cars behind him. After about 20 laps, he had settled into a rhythm. Jim Clark, the British driver in the lead car, sped away from the rest of the field. Parnelli Jones held on to second place. Andretti tried to catch up with Jones but came across the finish line six seconds behind the veteran driver. Still, Andretti's third-place finish easily won him the award for Indy Rookie of the Year.

His strong finish at Indy was just the beginning of a phenomenal season for the young driver. He won only one race, a 150-mile road race at Indianapolis Raceway Park, but he performed strongly in many races, including second place finishes at the Langhorne 100, the Atlanta 200, the Milwaukee 150, and the Phoenix 200. Andretti became the first rookie to win the USAC national championship since 1949.

CAREER UPS AND DOWNS

Hot off of his championship season, Andretti started the 1966 season with high hopes. But in the first race of the season, he and A.J. Foyt were battling for the lead and crashed into each other while trying to pass slower traffic. Bad luck continued to haunt Andretti. At the Indy 500, he qualified for the pole position at 165.899 mph but had to drop out of the race in the seventeenth lap when a twisted rod trashed the engine.

Mario Andretti experiences some bad luck at the 1966 USAC Championship time trials in Langhorne, Pennsylvania. Andretti's car slides sideways *(top left)*, then slams into the guardrail going backward *(bottom)*, and finishes with a spinout *(top right)* and collapsed left front wheel.

But the tide soon turned. Andretti led the next three races—the Milwaukee 100, Atlanta 300, and Langhorne 100. He then won a road race at the Indianapolis Raceway Park for his fourth victory in a row. Later in the season he won the Milwaukee 200 and the Trenton 200. To top it all off, Andretti clinched his second national title and then won his final race of the year, the Phoenix 200.

After two straight national championships, Andretti felt like the king of the racing world. He won the 1967

Daytona 500, the biggest race of the **NASCAR** circuit. Behind the wheel of a Ford Fairlane, he grabbed the lead for good at the 200-mile mark and pushed the stock car around the 2.5-mile oval to take the checkered flag. He followed up this victory with an endurance race in Sebring, Florida. In a Ford Mark N, Andretti and codriver Bruce McLaren covered 2,376 miles in 12 hours, breaking the old speed record in addition to snagging the victory. Then in the 1967 Indy 500, Andretti captured the pole position with a record speed of 167.942 mph. But on race day, he lost a wheel on lap 58 and ended up in thirtieth place.

Following his disappointment at Indy, Andretti drove in the legendary 24-hour endurance race in Le Mans, France. An error by the pit crew caused his car's brakes to fail and he broke his rib in the resulting crash. After the injury, Andretti came back to earn six victories, winning the 150-mile road race at Indianapolis Raceway Park for

The enduringly popular Mario Andretti takes his 1967 pole-sitting car for a ceremonial lap around the track before practice for the 90th running of the Indianapolis 500 in May, 2006.

the third year in a row, a 150-mile race in Langhorne, Pennsylvania and 200-mile races in Milwaukee, Wisconsin; Phoenix, Arizona; and St. Jovite, Canada. Entering the last race of the season, a 300-mile race at Riverside Park Speedway in Massachusetts, Andretti stood in second place behind A.J. Foyt and was within reach of a third national championship. Andretti ended up finishing the race in third place. Foyt finished fifth, however, and won the USAC championship.

Before the 1968 season began, Al Dean, owner of the Dean Van Lines racing team, passed away and Andretti bought the team. Although his car had a new, turbo-charged Ford engine, Andretti had a string of poor finishes. The new engine provided a lot of power, but it slowed down coming out of corners and had overheating problems. Andretti substituted an older Ford engine into his car while the Ford engineers worked to improve the new engine before the Indy 500. With the old engine, he finished second in the Trenton 150 in April.

THE 24 HOURS AT LE MANS

The world's most famous endurance race is held each June near Le Mans, France. The race traditionally starts at four o'clock on a Saturday afternoon. Each team of drivers—there are now three drivers to a team—races their car around an eight-mile circuit. The car that covers the most distance in 24 hours wins. The Le Mans track consists mostly of normal roads, with a few sections of track built specifically for the race. Winners at Le Mans have included such legendary drivers as Phil Hill, A.J. Foyt, Jacky Ickx, and Derek Bell. Le Mans is the only major race that Andretti never won.

At the 1968 Indy 500, there was a battle over the new generation of turbine engines, a battle that overshadowed the race itself. Many owners wanted turbine engines banned. Seeking a compromise, the USAC rules committee placed a size limitation on the turbines, which lowered the engines' performance. Andretti qualified in fourth place but burned out a piston in the first lap of the race. He jumped into the team's second car, which was being driven by Larry Dickson, but after 28 laps, the engine in that car also burned out.

Andretti finished second in six of the next nine races and he won the Trenton 200. After steadily racking up

Mario Andretti steps out of his car after competing in his first drag race. For a change of pace, he tried drag racing at the Connecticut Dragway in May, 1968, and won three out of five races. A few days later he competed in the Indianapolis 500.

Mario Andretti drives the number 4 Lotus Ford, and leads the pack from his pole position for the start of the 1969 Grand Prix in Sebring, Florida.

points in the national championship race, he went into the final race of the season in Riverside with the most points. He was followed by the Unser brothers, Bobby and Al. Andretti's car developed engine troubles, and he finished way back in the pack. Bobby Unser finished second and won the national championship, beating Andretti by 11 points.

Before the 1969 season began, the well-known team owner Andy Granatelli offered to buy Andretti's team. Tired of all the headaches involved with being the team's owner, Andretti gladly accepted. The new team planned to race a Ford-powered Lotus, but the car would not be ready for the start of the season. So Andretti drove his old car, a Hawk that was powered by a Ford turbo engine. At the Phoenix 150, the first race of the 1969 season, Andretti had driven only 29 laps when he had to withdraw from the race with a burned-out clutch. He bounced back by winning the next event, a 200-mile race in Hanford. It was Andy Granatelli's first championship victory as an owner in his 23 years of racing.

The new Lotus arrived in time for the month-long preparation for the Indy 500. Many racing insiders thought that Andretti was a lock to win the race. On the final day of practice, however, a rear wheel flew off the car and Andretti crashed into the wall. Although he suffered burns on his face, the determined driver returned to the track in the Hawk the next day in order to qualify for the second starting position. Although the car had some problems with its engine cooling system, Andretti won the race easily after other top contenders dropped out or fell behind early.

A THIRD CHAMPIONSHIP

With the Indy victory under his belt, Andretti began the quest to win his third USAC national championship. On June 29, he competed in the unusual 12-mile Pike's Peak hill climb—a wild and woolly race up a treacherous, windy mountain road to the top of Colorado's most famous mountain. Behind the wheel of a Chevy, Andretti streaked up the mountainside and won the race.

He then returned to Nazareth for Mario Andretti Day. The town threw a rollicking two-hour parade to honor its favorite son. Later, at a party at his house, Andretti jokingly commented, "Many people here in town thought I'd never amount to anything. Maybe they were right. . . . Here I am at twenty-nine and I still don't have a steady job."

At the Trenton 300, Andretti edged out Bobby Unser to win his twenty-sixth championship race. The victory assured him of his third USAC championship, but he still had something to prove. The final race of the season was the Rex Mays 300 in Riverside, California. He had never won on that track, and with the national championship already in his back pocket Andretti was determined to win this time. He staged a thrilling come-from-behind sprint and pulled away at the end to win by 37 seconds. The victory capped Andretti's finest year yet.

5

🏁

THE MAN WHO COULD WIN ANY KIND OF RACE

For Andretti, the highlight of the 1970 season was the grueling noon-to-midnight race in Sebring, the oldest endurance race in the United States. He had won the race in 1967, but this year was special because the Italian-born Andretti was driving for Team Ferrari. Andretti put the Italian sports car on the pole position with a record qualifying speed of 121.954 mph. Alternating with Italian driver Arturo Merzario, Andretti held off Peter Revson to take the checkered flag in the end.

A FORMULA 1 DREAM BECOMES A REALITY

The following year, Andretti began to pursue his lifelong dream, racing on the international Grand Prix circuit, also known as **Formula 1** (F1) racing. The Grand Prix circuit consists of 16 races held over 10 months. It takes place on four continents and provides the ultimate test of a driver's skill and courage. Andretti had previously raced in two F1

Mario Andretti sends out a spray of water from a rain-slicked track as he races his Formula 1 Ferrari during the 1971 Monaco Grand Prix in Monte Carlo.

races but had not finished strongly. He decided to devote more of his time to the Grand Prix circuit.

His concentrated effort paid off. He won two F1 races in 1971: the South African Grand Prix in Kyalami and a Grand Prix race in Ontario, California. That same year Andretti parted company with Andy Granatelli and joined a new USAC racing team put together by former driver Parnelli Jones. The two other drivers on the team were Al Unser and Joe Leonard. Racing writers dubbed it "the dream team," but the high expectations were never met. The cars did not run very well, and the three stars never found their way to Victory Lane.

Andretti left Jones's team in 1976 to join the Grand Prix circuit full time, though he occasionally drove in USAC races for the Roger Penske team. Andretti signed with Colin Chapman, whose Lotus team was building a new F1 car—the Lotus 79. Andretti had driven for Lotus in his first Grand Prix race in 1968. He had great respect for Chapman's abilities as a car builder and team manager.

The Lotus 79 was not close to being ready for the 1976 season, so Andretti climbed into the cockpit of the existing Lotus model. Even though he was driving an older car, he finished in sixth place in the 1976 Grand Prix points standings and won one event, the Japanese Grand Prix. In 1977, Andretti continued driving the older Lotus while testing the Lotus 79. He won four Grand Prix races in 1977—in

THE LEGENDARY LOTUS

Colin Chapman caught the racing bug as an engineering student at the University College of London. He started the Lotus Engineering Company in 1952. Using aircraft construction methods that he learned in college, he designed and built cars that won races around the world. Team Lotus's first Formula 1 victory came at the Grand Prix at Monaco in 1960, with Stirling Moss at the wheel. Jim Clark later steered a Lotus to win the 1965 Indianapolis 500. From 1960 to 1980, Lotus dominated Formula 1 racing. Clark, Graham Hill, Jochen Rindt, Emerson Fittipaldi, and Andretti all won world championships driving for Team Lotus. After Chapman's death in 1982, ownership of the company changed hands several times. Ayrton Senna captured Lotus's last Formula 1 victory in 1987.

Spain, France, Italy, and Long Beach, California—and finished third in the year's point championship.

The 1978 Grand Prix season proved to be not only Andretti's greatest year, but also one of the greatest years any F1 racer has ever had. He won the first race of the season in Argentina and then swept through the European events in Belgium, Spain, France, and Germany. He also placed second in Long Beach, California, and fourth in Brazil. Despite this impressive achievement, he did not have the season championship sewn up. Andretti had earned 54 points going into the Holland Grand Prix and several other top drivers were still in the running.

Andretti's closest competitor, however, was his teammate Ronnie Peterson. All year, the Swedish driver had been the ultimate team player. He would drive at the same speed as Andretti and block other cars from getting around him whenever Andretti was in the lead. Although the team owner gave Peterson the green light to win only when Andretti's car had broken down, Peterson had won the Austrian and Japanese Grand Prix races. Peterson had also finished strongly in several other races. Now, with only four races left in the season, the number two driver on the Lotus team had 45 points and was in a position to win the season championship himself.

At the Holland Grand Prix, Andretti finally found himself behind the wheel of the Lotus 79. He had no choice because he had crashed the older Lotus two weeks earlier at the Austrian Grand Prix. The Lotus 79 was a gem, and Andretti captured the pole position. On race day, he zoomed off and built up a comfortable lead. Peterson, running in second place, continued to be a team player. Although he had several opportunities to challenge

Andretti and his Formula 1 teammate, friend, and closest competitor, Ronnie Peterson *(right)*, prepare to race in the 1978 British Grand Prix in Brands Hatch, England. Peterson was hailed as the ultimate team player for keeping other racers off of Andretti's tail, enabling Andretti to win races.

Andretti for the lead, he concentrated on keeping other racers—especially Carlos Reutemann and Niki Lauda—off Andretti's tail. Andretti charged to the finish line, capturing the checkered flag and nine more precious Grand Prix points. He also took one giant step toward becoming the first American to win the F1 points championship since Phil Hill had won it in 1961.

Andretti could capture the championship at the race in Monza, Italy, on September 10. He won the pole position and, when the race began, he pushed the Lotus 79 into the lead. Behind him, however, disaster had struck.

Andretti leads the field, and Peterson is a close second, in the first lap of the 1978 Dutch Formula One Grand Prix. That was the order in which they finished, which gave Andretti the 1978 Formula 1 World Championship.

Seconds into the race, 10 cars crashed and tangled into a fiery pile. Ronnie Peterson, starting in the fifth slot, was among the drivers involved. The race was stopped while all the twisted wreckage was removed from the course. An ambulance rushed Peterson to the hospital. Reports indicated at first that he had suffered multiple leg injuries. Doctors felt certain that he would recover. The race restarted after a three-hour delay and Andretti cruised around the course and sped across the finish line in first place.

Mario Andretti crosses the finish line first in the 1978 Italian Grand Prix in Monza, Italy, only to be penalized for jumping the start. He was officially listed as the sixth place finisher in the tragic race that would ultimately cost his teammate Ronnie Peterson's life.

When Andretti walked to the judge's stand to claim the Monza Cup, he learned that he and the second-place finisher, Gilles Villeneuve of Canada, were being penalized one minute each for starting too early at the restart of the race. The judges gave third-place finisher Niki Lauda the winner's trophy. Andretti then learned that, even though he did not win the race, he had clinched the season title. But there was little else to celebrate. Because of his injuries, Peterson would miss the final two races of the season, and after that his health grew worse. Despite the optimistic diagnosis doctors first gave him, Peterson

Andretti walks with his wife, Dee Ann, at the Daytona Motor Speedway, in Daytona, Florida, circa 1980.

slipped into a coma and died of kidney failure. Andretti was devastated. He and Peterson had been good friends and perfect teammates.

HURT BY CAR TROUBLES

After winning the F1 championship, Andretti kept doing what he did best—racing. The victories, however, began to come with less frequency. He continued to drive on the Formula 1 circuit, winning the Meadowlands Grand Prix in 1984 and the Long Beach Grand Prix in 1985. During this time, though, his bad luck at Indy continued. In 1981, track officials awarded him the victory when first-place finisher Bobby Unser was punished for passing cars under a **yellow flag**. Unser argued against the ruling, which was eventually reversed, and Andretti's victory was taken away. The following year, Andretti found himself in the cockpit of a fast car but a crash at

Andretti stops for gas during the 1985 Toyota Grand Prix in Long Beach, California. He led the race for 70 laps and won by a lead of one minute.

the start of the race knocked him out of the running. His teammate, Gordon Johncock, captured the checkered flag in an identical car.

In the 1985 Indy, racer Danny Sullivan was in the lead when his car went out of control and spun wildly. Andretti avoided Sullivan's spinning car and led Indy for 102 laps. But Sullivan managed to avoid hitting anything and roared back to take the lead from Andretti, winning the race. Andretti finished in second place again. It was so

The tail of Danny Sullivan's car slides out as he exits a turn, causing him to spin around in front of Mario Andretti. Andretti avoids hitting Sullivan and Sullivan miraculously avoids hitting the wall, allowing each driver to continue the race. Sullivan later passes Andretti at the same spot, becoming the first driver ever to "spin and win."

close to his second Indy win, yet so far away. Then in 1987, Andretti led Indy for 170 laps when his engine failed. Six years later, in 1993, Andretti was on the road to victory once again. He led for 72 laps, but a bad tire dropped him to a fifth-place finish.

6

THE ANDRETTI LEGACY

By 1990, Andretti was entering his fourth decade of racing. Although still competitive, he began to pass the torch to a new generation of Andrettis who wanted to keep the family name in Victory Lane. Mario's sons, Michael and Jeff, and Aldo's son, John, all caught the racing bug and became world-class drivers. Mario's grandson Marco also quickly made a name for himself as a driver.

The 1992 USAC season proved to be an exceptional showcase for the Andrettis. At every Indy car race that year, there were four Andrettis in the field. All four qualified for the Indy 500. Two years later, Mario and Michael shared a special moment. At the 1994 Australian Indy Car Grand Prix, father and son finished first and third. Michael won the race, but Mario showed everyone that he was still a competitor.

Growing up, Michael had watched his father race many times. In his 1993 book *Michael Andretti at Indianapolis*, he recalled, "Ever since I was a child, racing has been the only thing I wanted to do." He claimed his first USAC

Mario Andretti's son Michael, an Indy Racing League driver and car owner, waits for the start of practice for the 2006 Indianapolis 500.

national championship in 1991. Like his father, he competed in many different cars and on many different race circuits, including Formula 1. Michael's career highlights include winning co-Rookie of the Year at the 1984 Indy 500 and capturing his first Indy car win in 1986. In 2003, Michael retired with 42 Indy car victories. That placed him third behind A.J. Foyt (67 wins) and his father (52 wins) for the number of victories won by any racer. Michael wanted to concentrate on Andretti Green Racing, the four-car racing team that he owned. He came out of retirement to drive in the 2006 Indianapolis 500 with his son Marco. In 2007, Michael's team featured drivers Marco Andretti and the first female driver to lead the Indy 500, Danica Patrick, a favorite among fans.

Jeff Andretti started winning go-kart events in 1981 and worked his way up to driving Indy cars in 1990. He was named Rookie of the Year at Indy in 1991, just as his father (in 1965) and brother (in 1984) had before him. The following year at Indy, however, a terrible crash ended his day on lap 109. Jeff spent three weeks in the hospital recovering. He returned to racing in 1993 but never reached the same level of success.

Aldo's son, John, also carries on the Andretti tradition. He won his first Indy car race in 1991. Like Mario Andretti, John has driven almost every type of race car, including midgets, Indy cars, and Formula 1 cars. In recent years, he has focused on the NASCAR circuit, driving for the respected Richard Petty, Dale Earnhardt, and ppc teams. He also makes many personal appearances to help raise money for such charities as the Riley Hospital for Children in Indianapolis.

The youngest racing Andretti, Marco, burst onto the scene in 2006. The 19-year-old driver thrilled fans at the 2006 Indy 500. Marco led the race after passing his father, Michael, with three laps remaining. On the final straightaway, however, Sam Hornish Jr. wove his faster car through a small opening between Marco's car and the inside wall. Hornish took the checkered flag, with Marco finishing 0.0635 seconds behind. It was the first time in the race's 90-year history that the lead changed hands in the final lap. Michael Andretti finished in third place.

In August 2006, Marco won the Indy Grand Prix of Sonoma, becoming the youngest driver to win a major

Aldo Andretti's son John, a NASCAR Busch series driver, awaits the start of the O'Reilly Challenge 300 race in Fort Worth, Texas, in November, 2006.

RACING FAMILIES

There have been several families who have dominated the racing world at one time or another. Families that have competed in the Indy 500 include the Bettenhausens, Chevrolets, Foyts, Mears, Rathmanns, Snevas, Unsers, and Vukovichs. In NASCAR, the Allison, Earnhardt, Jarrett, Petty, and Waltrip families have been frequent visitors to Victory Lane. Of these legendary racing families, the Andrettis have been the most successful.

Michael Andretti's son Marco carries on the family's racing tradition. Mario Andretti is shown embracing Marco after he won the 2006 IRL IndyCar Series Grand Prix at the Infineon Raceway in Sonoma, California. Marco drove the number 26 Andretti Green Racing NYSE Dallara Honda for his first IndyCar race win.

Indy race. His father was 23 years old when he won at Long Beach in 1986, and his grandfather Mario was 25 years old when he won the Hoosier Grand Prix in 1965. At the end of the 2006 season, the Indy Racing League named Marco its Rookie of the Year. When asked about his racing future, Marco showed the Andretti competitive spirit, vowing, "My goal is to be better than both of them," referring to his father and grandfather. Mario summed up his family's attraction to racing: "We just love to drive. We love race cars. We just love to do it. We were born to do it, I think."

READY FOR RETIREMENT

Before the 1994 season, Mario Andretti announced that it would be his last season as a driver. At about the same time, *Car and Driver* magazine named him as one of the top 10 American drivers of all time. As the 54-year-old veteran took his final spins around the racetracks of the world, many fans got their last glimpses at the racing legend. The winner of three USAC national champion-ships and a Formula 1 world championship, Andretti had scored victories on a wide array of tracks in a wide variety of cars. He won sprint car and midget races on dirt tracks. He won stock car races on paved oval tracks. He won championship and road races in Indy cars. He won endurance races in sports cars, and Grand Prix races in Formula 1 cars. Mario Andretti is enshrined in three halls of fame: the Indianapolis 500, the Sprint Car, and the Motor Sports.

But retirement from racing did not slow him down. He continued to hang out in racing circles. He even tested cars for Michael Andretti's team. In 1996 he climbed back

Retirement did not slow down Mario Andretti. As the
featured driver in a movie about IndyCar racing, Andretti
drives around the track at the 1996 Toronto IndyCar race
with an IMAX camera attached to the car.

in a race car to star in the IMAX film *Super Speedway*. He still received offers to drive in the 24 Hours of Le Mans, the only major auto race he had not won. Then, in 2003, he smashed up one of Michael's test cars. The car hit some debris on the track, went airborne, and cartwheeled down the track. Although he was not hurt, the terrifying crash finally convinced him to put away the driving gloves.

Following his retirement, Andretti has pursued various business ventures and won many awards and honors. He owns a car dealership, a chain of gas stations, car washes, go-kart tracks, a California winery, and several other business enterprises. He makes public appearances for Texaco and accepts many requests to speak to corporate audiences. In October 2004, he served as grand marshal of New York City's Columbus Day Parade, which honors Italian Americans. In February 2006, Andretti attended the closing ceremonies of the Winter Olympics in Torino, Italy, as part of the official U.S. delegation. In October 2006, he was awarded the title of Commendatore della Repubblica Italiana by Italy's consul general in a ceremony in New York City. The award recognized his outstanding career and personality, which provided a positive image of Italians throughout the world. (The title is given by the Ordine al Merito della Repubblica, an organization similar to the United Kingdom's Order of the British Empire.) Andretti still lives in Nazareth with his wife, Dee Ann. The street he lives on has been renamed Victory Lane.

As older drivers pass the torch to a new generation of drivers, some racing fans doubt that the younger stars will ever attain the legendary status of Mario Andretti and the

Mario Andretti sports his winning smile and the medal he received at the Columbus Citizens Foundation in October, 2006. Andretti earned the title of Commendatore, the highest honor granted a civilian by the Italian government.

other great names in racing. In an era of large monetary prizes for winning races, friendship and trust among drivers have diminished. Auto racing seems to boast fewer original personalities. Some fans even argue that much of the romance of the sport seems to have faded. But what will never fade are the accomplishments of the man who could win any kind of race: Mario Andretti.

STATISTICS

HIGHLIGHTS OF MARIO ANDRETTI'S FOUR CHAMPIONSHIP SEASONS

1965 USAC CHAMPIONSHIP

Date	Track	Distance	Finish
April 25	Trenton	100	2
May 31	Indianapolis	500	3
June 20	Langhorne	100	2
July 25	Indianapolis Raceway Park	150	1
August 1	Atlanta	300	2
August 14	Milwaukee	150	2
August 21	Springfield	100	3
September 18	Indianapolis Fairgrounds	100	2
October 24	Sacramento	100	3
November 11	Phoenix	200	2

1966 USAC CHAMPIONSHIP

Date	Track	Distance	Finish
June 5	Milwaukee	100	1
June 12	Langhorne	100	1
June 26	Atlanta	300	1
July 24	Indianapolis Raceway Park	150	1
August 20	Springfield	100	2
August 27	Milwaukee	200	1
September 10	Indianapolis Fairgrounds	100	1
September 25	Trenton	200	1
November 20	Phoenix	200	1

1969 USAC CHAMPIONSHIP

Date	Track	Distance	Finish
April 13	Hanford	200	1
May 30	Indianapolis	500	1
June 29	Pike's Peak	12.5	1
July 19	Trenton	200	1
July 27	Indianapolis Raceway Park	100	2
August 18	Springfield	100	1
September 1	DuQuoin	100	2
September 21	Trenton	300	1
December 7	Riverside	300	1

1978 FORMULA 1 CHAMPIONSHIP

Date	Event, Site	Finish
January	Argentina Grand Prix, Buenos Aires	1
April	Spanish G.P., Jarama	1
May	Belgium G.P., Spa-Fransorchamps	1
July	French G.P., Le Mans	1
August	Holland G.P., Zandvoort	1
September	Italian G.P., Monza	3

CHRONOLOGY

1940   Mario and brother Aldo are born on February 28 in Montona, Italy.

1948   The Andrettis leave Montona and settle in a refugee camp in Italy.

1955   The Andrettis arrive in the United States on June 16.

1959   Mario and Aldo begin racing at Nazareth Speedway.

1961   Marries Dee Ann Hoch on November 25.

1964   Wins first USAC race, a 100-mile sprint race at Salem, Indiana; becomes U.S. citizen on April 15.

1965   Wins USAC national points championship; named Rookie of the Year at Indianapolis 500.

1966   Wins second USAC national championship.

1967   Finishes second in USAC national championship; wins Daytona 500 and 12 Hours at Sebring endurance race.

1968   Finishes second in USAC national championship; drives in first Formula 1 race.

1969   Wins third USAC national championship; wins Indy 500.

1970   Wins second 12 Hours at Sebring.

1971   Wins two Formula 1 races.

1976   Wins Japanese Grand Prix.

1977   Wins four Formula 1 races.

1978   Wins six Formula 1 races and the Grand Prix points championship.

1981   Awarded Indy 500 victory when judges strip Bobby Unser of title; awarded second place after Unser's successful protest.

1984   Wins Meadowlands Grand Prix.

1985   Finishes second at Indy 500; wins Long Beach Grand Prix.

1992   Four Andrettis—Mario, Michael, Jeff, and John— qualify for Indy 500.

1994   Michael and Mario finish first and third, respectively, at the Australian Indy Car Grand Prix; Mario Andretti retires from racing.

1996   Mario and Michael Andretti star in the IMAX film *Super Speedway*.

2004   Mario serves as grand marshal of New York City's Columbus Day Parade.

2006   Marco Andretti and Michael Andretti finish second and third, respectively, in the Indy 500; Marco wins his first Indy Racing League race and is named IRL Rookie of the Year; Mario Andretti attends the closing ceremonies of the Winter Olympics in Torino, Italy, and is honored as a Commendatore della Repubblica Italiana.

GLOSSARY

Checkered flag—the flag that is waved when the winner of a race crosses the finish line

Circuit—a planned schedule of car races for a certain racing organization

Formula 1—grand prix racing, consisting of road races throughout the world

Lap—one complete circuit around a racetrack

Midget car (midget racer)—a race car that is very small and usually driven in short-distance races

NASCAR—the National Association for Stock Car Auto Racing, the organization that oversees stock car races (and other types of races)

Pit stop—a short stop during a race in which a driver pulls over to refuel and allow the crew to make repairs

Pole position—the number-one starting position, usually earned by having the fastest car during qualifying rounds

Qualifying round—a system of timed practice runs held before races, used to establish which drivers are eligible for the race and to determine the drivers' positions on the starting grid

Sprint car—small, powerful race cars

Stock car—race cars that have similar bodies to automobiles sold to the general public: NASCAR racing cars

White flag—the flag that is waved when the leader of the race has one lap remaining

Yellow flag—the flag that is waved when there is a hazard on the racetrack, such as an accident, debris, or a wet surface; drivers must slow down and are not permitted to pass another car

BIBLIOGRAPHY

Andretti, Mario. *What's It Like Out There?* Chicago: Henry Regnery Co., 1970.

Andretti, Michael. *Michael Andretti at Indianapolis.* New York: Simon & Schuster, 1993.

Associated Press Sports Staff. *A Century of Champions.* New York: Macmillan, 1976.

Crombac, Gerard. *Colin Chapman: The Man and His Cars.* Newbury Park, Calif.: Haynes, 2002.

Engel, Lyle Kenyon. *Mario Andretti.* New York: Arco, 1979.

Engel, Lyle Kenyon. *Road Racing in America.* New York: Dodd, Mead, 1971.

Higham, Peter. *International Motor Racing Guide.* London: David Bull, 1993.

Hinton, Ed. "Inherit the Wind." *Sports Illustrated*, May 11, 1992.

Leifer, Neil. *Neil Leifer's Sports Stars.* Garden City, N.Y.: Dolphin Books, 1985.

Libby, Bill. *Andretti: The Story of Auto-Racing's Toughest, Most Versatile and Courageous Driver.* New York: Grosset & Dunlap, 1970.

Roebuck, Nigel. *Grand Prix Greats.* Wellingborough, U.K.: Patrick Stevens, 1986.

Super Speedway: http://www.superspeedway.com

Sutton, Stan. "Destiny's Darling Andretti Ain't." *The Sporting News*, June 1, 1987.

FURTHER READING

Fish, Bruce, and Becky Durost Fish. *Indy Car Racing.* Langhorne, Pa.: Chelsea House, 2001.

Gillespie, Tom, ed. *Racing Families: A Tribute to Racing's Fastest Dynasties.* Dallas, Tex.: Beckett, 2000.

Golenbock, Peter, ed. *NASCAR Encyclopedia.* St. Paul, Minn.: Motorbooks International, 2003.

Herren, Joe, and Ron Thomas. *Formula One Car Racing.* Langhorne, Pa.: Chelsea House, 2003.

Martin, James A., and Thomas F. Saal. *American Auto Racing: The Milestones and Personalities of a Century of Speed.* Jefferson, N.C.: McFarland, 2004.

McGuire. *The History of NASCAR.* Langhorne, Pa.: Chelsea House, 2000.

Minard, Pierre. *The Great Encyclopedia of Formula 1.* St. Paul, Minn.: Motorbooks International, 2001.

WEB SITES

www.andretti.com
Official Web site of the Andretti family.

www.andrettigreenracing.com
Michael Andretti's racing team of the Indy Racing League Indy Car Series.

www.marcoandretti.com
Web site of racing newcomer Marco Andretti.

www.formula1.com
Official Web site of specialty Formula 1 racing.

www.brickyard.com
Indianapolis Motor Speedway's official site.

www.nascar.com
Information covering the NASCAR racing series.

PICTURE CREDITS

INDEX

ABOUT THE AUTHOR

G.S. PRENTZAS is an editor and writer who lives in New York. He has written a dozen books for young readers, including a guide to the 1994 Winter Olympics and a biography of football great Jim Brown. He is also the co-author of *A.J. Foyt* in Chelsea House's RACE CAR LEGENDS: COLLECTOR'S EDITION series.